Consider it Golf

Golf etiquette and safety tips for children!

by Susan Greene

Illustrations by Dagne Angersbach Klavins

Excel Publishing

Troy, Michigan

For my family, Dave and Jamie, thanks for the joy!

S.G.

To my good friend Dick Nichol, eye surgeon Dr. James M. Weisz and my dear husband Uldis, who each in very different ways were instrumental in my decision to illustrate this book.

D.A.K.

From the start of the day, to the end of your play,
Be considerate and polite every step of the way!

If you make a divot when you hit the ball,
Be sure to follow protocol!
If a soil and seed mixture is around,
Use it to fill the hole in the ground.

If not, take the divot in your hand,
And do your best to restore the land.
Return the divot and tap it in place,
As unrepaired divots are a disgrace!

If you make a ball mark on the green,
Repair it so it can't be seen.
And if a group ahead forgot this chore,
Then do your best to repair some more!

Sun safety is a big concern.
Please wear sunscreen so you don't burn!!!

If you hit towards others,
Warn them with a shout.

Holler "FORE" real loud
So they will lookout!

When going in and out of a bunker,
There is a general guide,
Be sure to enter and exit
From the low side!

If you enter a bunker,
There's an extra step to take.
Make sure each and every footprint
Disappears with a rake!

When removing the flagstick from the hole,
Be sure to keep it in control.
Don't throw or toss it on the ground.
Just set it down gently without a sound!

When you are on the green,
Expectations are clear-cut.
Walk around and not on
A player's line of putt!

Your exit from the green shouldn't begin
Until the last putt of your group rolls in!!

Once a player grabs a club
On the course or practice tee,
Keep your distance when they swing
To avoid an injury!!

The game of golf is not a race,
But do your best to keep the pace.

Be prepared to hit when it's your turn
So keeping up won't be a concern!

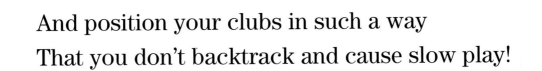

And position your clubs in such a way
That you don't backtrack and cause slow play!

If you hit a bad shot,
Please stay calm and cool.
Because if you throw your club,
You just look like a fool!
And besides looking foolish,
You could hurt someone,
And that would take away
From all your golfing fun!

When you finish playing golf,
Whether you win or lose,

Before entering the clubhouse,
Clean your spikes and shoes!

If you win a trophy,
There are a few things you should do.
Please smile, shake hands and say thank you!

No singing!
No whistling!
No tapping your toes!
Keep quiet while others hit
Be it amateurs or pros!

Sometimes you may walk,
And other times you'll ride.
But if you see lightning,
Go directly inside!

You wouldn't hit here,
The group ahead is too near.
Wait until they finish
For the fairway to clear!

HOLE 14

Compliment good shots throughout the day.
"Great shot" or "Good putt" is something you can say.

And help others search for balls gone astray.

Let playing partners know that you had fun,
By telling them so when the day is done.
"I enjoyed playing with you!" Or "I had a great day!"
Are just a couple of things that you might say.
Please keep in mind, from beginning to end,
Be a good sport and be a good friend!

A quick review and then you are through.
Which statements are **false** and which are **true**?

1. Golfers should repair their divots.

2. Ball marks should not be repaired.

3. Wear sunscreen to protect your skin.

4. Holler "FORE" when you make a putt.

5. Enter bunkers from the low side.

6. Footprints should be left in the bunker.

7. Let flagsticks drop to the ground.

8. Do not walk on a player's line of putt.

9. Do not exit the green until everyone in your
   group has finished putting.

10. Keep your distance from other golfers
    preparing to swing.

11. Be prepared to hit when it is your turn.

12. Do not throw your clubs.

13. Do not clean your shoes and spikes before entering the clubhouse.

14. Smile, shake hands and say thank you when receiving a trophy.

15. It is okay to whistle while others are hitting.

16. Go directly inside if you see lightning.

17. Do not hit into a group in front of you.

18. It is nice to compliment good shots.

19. Do not help others search for balls gone astray.

20. Be a good sport.

Answers

1. True
2. False, ball marks should be repaired.
3. True
4. False, holler "FORE" as a warning when you hit towards others.
5. True
6. False, rake your footprints in the bunker.
7. False, set flagsticks down gently.
8. True
9. True
10. True
11. True
12. True
13. False, shoes and spikes should be cleaned before entering the clubhouse.
14. True
15. False, keep quiet while others are hitting.
16. True
17. True
18. True
19. False, help others search for balls gone astray.
20. True

Golf etiquette and safety should be more familiar now,
So practice them when you play now that you know how!

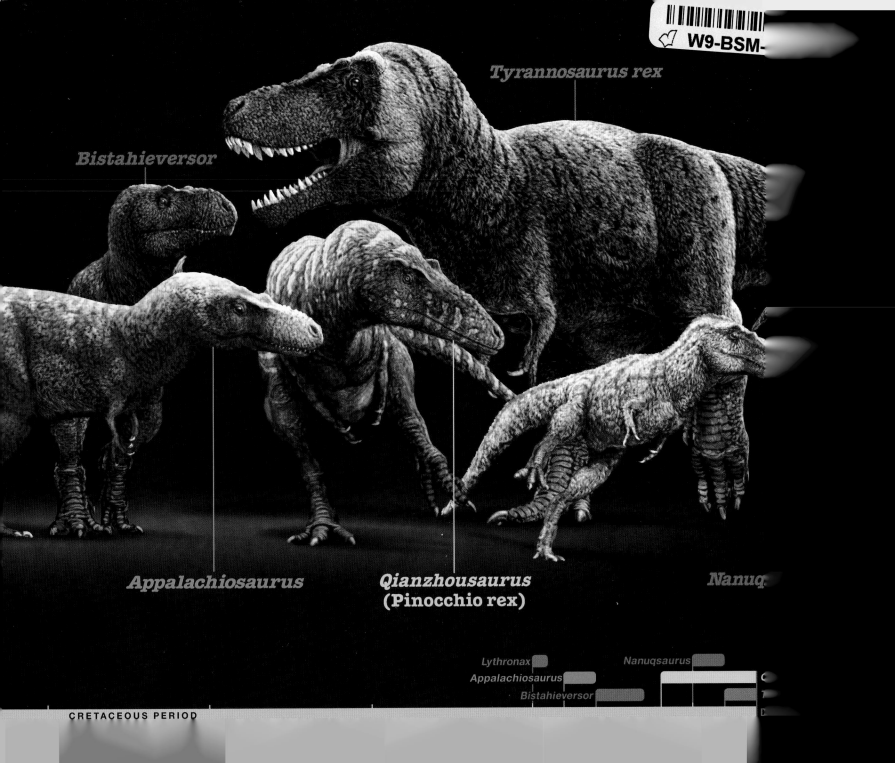

Tyrannosaurus rex

Bistahieversor

Appalachiosaurus

Qianzhousaurus
(Pinocchio rex)

Nanuq.

Lythronax

Nanuqsaurus

Appalachiosaurus

Bistahieversor

CRETACEOUS PERIOD

PINOCCHIO REX AND OTHER TYRANNOSAURS

BY MELISSA STEWART & STEVE BRUSATTE

ILLUSTRATED BY JULIUS CSOTONYI

HARPER

An Imprint of HarperCollinsPublishers

*For Steve Brusatte, a great scientist and
a great collaborator*—M.S.

*For my wife, Anne, and all of her fellow
school teachers everywhere*—S.B.

*For my wife, Alexandra, my joint adventurer
in life, scientific outreach, and art*—J.C.

The Let's-Read-and-Find-Out Science book series was originated by Dr. Franklyn M. Branley, Astronomer Emeritus and former Chairman of the American Museum–Hayden Planetarium, and was formerly co-edited by him and Dr. Roma Gans, Professor Emeritus of Childhood Education, Teachers College, Columbia University. Text and illustrations for each of the books in the series are checked for accuracy by an expert in the relevant field. For more information about Let's-Read-and-Find-Out Science books, write to HarperCollins Children's Books, 195 Broadway, New York, NY 10007, or visit our website at www.letsreadandfindout.com.

Let's Read-and-Find-Out Science® is a trademark of HarperCollins Publishers.
Pinocchio Rex and Other Tyrannosaurs
Text copyright © 2017 by Melissa Stewart and Steve Brusatte
Illustrations by Julius Csotonyi
Illustrations copyright © 2017 by HarperCollins Publishers
All rights reserved. Manufactured in China.
No part of this book may be used or reproduced in any manner whatsoever without written permission except in the case of brief quotations embodied in critical articles and reviews. For information address HarperCollins Children's Books, a division of HarperCollins Publishers, 195 Broadway, New York, NY 10007.
www.harpercollinschildrens.com

Library of Congress Control Number: 2017932854
ISBN 978-0-06-249093-3 (trade bdg.) — ISBN 978-0-06-249091-9 (pbk.)

The artist used a stylus and a drawing tablet to create the digital illustrations for this book.
Typography by Erica De Chavez 17 18 19 20 21 SCP 10 9 8 7 6 5 4 3 2 1 ❖ First Edition

You'll meet a lot of amazing dinosaurs in this book.
Here's how to say their names.

Appalachiosaurus • • • (ah-pah-LAY-chee-oh-SORE-us)

Bistahieversor • • • • • • • • • • (bis-TAH-hee-e-ver-sore)

Dilong • • • • • • • • • • • • • • • • • • • (DEE-long)

Eotyrannus • • • • • • • • • • • • • (EE-oh-tih-RAN-us)

Guanlong • • • • • • • • • • • • • • • • (GWON-long)

Kileskus • • • • • • • • • • • • • • • (kih-LESS-kuss)

Lythronax • • • • • • • • • • • • • • (LITH-roh-nax)

Nanuqsaurus • • • • • • • • • (nah-nook-SORE-us)

Qianzhousaurus • • • • • • • (SHAHN-zhoo-SORE-us)

Tyrannosaurus rex • • • • • (tie-RAN-uh-SORE-us REKS)

Yutyrannus • • • • • • • • • • • • (you-tih-RAN-us)

Why is *Tyrannosaurus rex* (tie-RAN-uh-SORE-us REKS) the most famous **dinosaur** of all time?

✔ Because it's so **BIG**. As big as a school bus.

✔ Because it's so **SCARY**. It had razor-sharp claws and teeth strong enough to crush bone.

✔ Because it's so **DIFFERENT** from anything alive today.

When the first *T. rex* **skeleton** went on display at the American Museum of Natural History in 1915, it took the world by storm. People had so many questions about **tyrannosaurs**.

When did they first live on Earth?

How had they changed over time?

Were they always so big?

For a long time, scientists didn't know the answers to any of these questions. But all that is starting to change.

What are we discovering? That the first tyrannosaurs were about the same size as us. It took almost 80 million years for them to become mighty beasts that ruled the land.

Dr. Steve Says

What's my favorite dinosaur? *T. rex!* I've been a fan since I was fifteen and helped my brother with a school project about the fearsome predator.

Tyrannosaurus rex

Discovery announced: 1905
Discovery site: United States
Size: 40 feet long, 15 feet tall, 15,000 pounds
Lived: 68–66 million years ago

On a hot summer day, a worker climbed
into a backhoe and started to dig a hole.

Scoop.
Lift.
Dump.
Scoop.
Lift.
Dump.

The red soil slowly piled up.

It seemed like a normal day. But then . . . *Crash!* The digger hit something big. Something hard. Something the worker never expected. When he jumped down, he spotted giant bones. Lots of them.

After studying the **fossils**, Dr. Steve had great news. They came from a brand-new kind of tyrannosaur! Its long snout could snap shut fast, so it probably caught small, speedy prey. And the row of horns on its snout may have helped it attract mates.

In 2014, the team announced their discovery. They named the dinosaur *Qianzhousaurus* (SHAHN-zhoo-SORE-us). But most of the time, they call it Pinocchio rex.

Dr. Steve Says

We named *Qianzhousaurus* after the part of China where it was found. But we thought it needed a nickname. The long snout made us think of Pinocchio's nose.

Pinocchio rex is just one of the many new tyrannosaurs scientists have discovered since 2000. Some of these dinosaurs lived around the same time as *T. rex* and Pinocchio rex, but others lived much earlier.

DINO FACT FILE

Qianzhousaurus

(nickname: Pinocchio rex)

Discovery announced: 2014
Discovery site: China
Size: 25 feet long, 7 feet tall, 2,000 pounds
Lived: 72–66 million years ago

Kileskus (kih-LESS-kuss) was one of the world's first tyrannosaurs. It was small and quick. *Kileskus* had long arms with three fingers on each hand.

Qianzhousaurus
Tyrannosaurus rex
DINOSAUR EXTINCTION

DINO FACT FILE

Kileskus

Discovery announced: 2010

Discovery site: Russia

Size: 9 feet long, 3 feet tall, 150 pounds

Lived: 168–166 million years ago

Guanlong

Discovery announced: 2006

Discovery site: China

Size: 9 feet long, 3 feet tall, 150 pounds

Lived: 164–157 million years ago

Kileskus · Guanlong

JURASSIC PERIOD

Guanlong (GWON-long) lived a few million years after *Kileskus*. It was small and had a huge, bony crest on its head. The crest may have helped it attract mates.

Dr. Steve Says

I love being the first person to see a dinosaur after it's been hidden away for millions of years. Some of my friends discovered *Guanlong* in the hot, dry desert of China. Just imagine how excited they must have been!

Qianzhousaurus
Tyrannosaurus rex
DINOSAUR EXTINCTION

Eotyrannus

Discovery announced: 2001

Discovery site: England

Size: 15 feet long, 4 feet tall, 400 pounds

Lived: 131–126 million years ago

Eotyrannus (EE-oh-tih-RAN-us) was alive at around the same time as *Yutyrannus* and *Dilong*. But it lived in a different part of the world.

Like other early tyrannosaurs, *Eotyrannus* had long arms. It could grab prey with the three long fingers on its hands.

Kileskus   *Guanlong*   *Eotyrannus*
                                        Dilong
                                        Yutyrannus

JURASSIC PERIOD

Dr. Steve Says

A dinosaur in England? Yep, it's true. The first time I saw *Eotyrannus*, I couldn't believe it. The bones looked a lot like a *T. rex*'s, but so much smaller.

Qianzhousaurus
Tyrannosaurus rex
DINOSAUR EXTINCTION

CRETACEOUS PERIOD

120   110   100   90   80   70   66

Lythronax

Discovery announced: 2013

Discovery site: United States

Size: 24 feet long, 7 feet tall, 5,000 pounds

Lived: 80 million years ago

About 90 million years ago, tyrannosaurs began to change. Over time, they grew bigger and heavier. The giant beasts had huge heads with bone-crushing teeth. They had tiny arms with just two fingers on each hand.

Eotyrannus

Dilong

Yutyrannus

Kileskus

Guanlong

JURASSIC PERIOD

170 million years ago   160   150   140   130

One of these mighty hunters was *Lythronax* (LITH-roh-nax).
It could catch and kill anything in its path. Scientists think that
a dinosaur like *Lythronax* developed into *T. rex*.

Qianzhousaurus
Tyrannosaurus rex
DINOSAUR EXTINCTION

Lythronax

CRETACEOUS PERIOD

120   110   100   90   80   70   66

Over the next 20 million years, many new kinds of tyrannosaurs appeared.
Pinocchio rex was one of them. So was *T. rex*. Here are a few others:

DINO FACT FILE

Appalachiosaurus

(ah-pah-LAY-chee-oh-SORE-us)

Discovery announced: 2005

Discovery site: United States

Size: 25 feet long, 7 feet tall,
2,000 pounds

Lived: 78–76 million years ago

DINO FACT FILE

Bistahieversor

(bis-TAH-hee-e-ver-sore)

Discovery announced: 2010

Discovery site: United States

Size: 25 feet long, 7 feet tall,
6,000 pounds

Lived: 76–73 million years ago

ileskus   Guanlong

JURASSIC PERIOD

Eotyrannus
Dilong
Yutyrannus

Dr. Steve Says

Bistahieversor was found in the badlands of New Mexico. I look for dinosaurs there every summer. I think it's one of the most beautiful places in the world.

DINO FACT FILE

Nanuqsaurus

(nah-nook-SORE-us)

Discovery announced: 2014
Discovery site: United States
Size: 18 feet long, 6 feet tall, 500 pounds
Lived: 70–68 million years ago

Lythronax
Nanuqsaurus
Appalachiosaurus
Qianzhousaurus
Bistahieversor
Tyrannosaurus rex

CRETACEOUS PERIOD
DINOSAUR EXTINCTION

110   100   90   80   70   66

About 66 million years ago, an **asteroid** smashed into Earth. Dust from the blast filled the sky. It blocked out the sun for years. Earth became a dark, cold place.

Plants couldn't grow. Most animals starved to death. *T. rex*, Pinocchio rex, and all the other dinosaurs disappeared forever.

If it weren't for fossils, we wouldn't know that tyrannosaurs had ever lived. So far scientists have dug up about twenty-five kinds of tyrannosaurs. Who knows how many more are waiting to be discovered.

31

MEET DR. STEVE

I grew up in Ottawa, Illinois, surrounded by cornfields. My brother Chris loved dinosaurs. When I helped him with a school project on *T. rex*, I was hooked.

I studied my first dinosaur when I was in college. It turned out to be a new species. Since then, I've identified ten new kinds of dinosaurs. I've studied other ancient animals too. But tyrannosaurs are still my favorite.

Me at age 15, collecting fossils at Mazon Creek in Illinois

Me, age 11, (middle) with my brothers Chris (left) and Mike (right)

Me and my wife, Anne

Studying Pinocchio rex bones

Today I live in Scotland with my wife, Anne. She's an elementary school teacher, and I'm a **paleontologist**. I spend part of my time teaching at the University of Edinburgh. The rest of the time I travel the world digging up and studying dinosaurs. It's a dream job.

HOW BIG WERE TYRANNOSAURS?

T. rex was one of the biggest hunters to ever live on land. But many tyrannosaurs re much smaller. To see how tyrannosaurs sized up, grab three colored pieces of lk and a tape measure. Then head out to the schoolyard or a local playground.

T. rex

Make a chalk mark on the pavement, and place a rock on top of it so you can easily see your starting point. Walk 40 feet to your right, and make a second chalk mark. Draw a line between the two marks to see how long *T. rex* was.

Now return to your first chalk mark, and walk 15 feet straight ahead. After making a second chalk mark, draw a line between the two marks to see how tall *T. rex* was. Complete the rectangle with two more lines and you'll see how big *T. rex* was. You may want to draw a figure that looks like *T. rex* inside the box.

Pinocchio rex

Using a different colored chalk, make a mark just to the right of the rock. Walk 25 feet to your right, and make another chalk mark. Draw a line between the two new marks to see how long Pinocchio rex was.

Now return to your first chalk mark, and walk 7 feet straight ahead. After making another chalk mark, draw a line between the two marks to see how tall Pinocchio rex was. Complete the rectangle with two more lines. Now you can compare the sizes of Pinocchio rex and *T. rex*. You may want to draw a figure that looks like Pinocchio rex inside the box.

Dilong

Using a third piece of chalk with a third color, make a mark just to the right of the Pinocchio rex chalk mark. Walk 5 feet to your right, and make another mark. Draw a line between the two marks to see how long *Dilong* was.

Now return to your first *Dilong* chalk mark, and walk 2 feet and 6 inches straight ahead. After making another chalk mark, draw a line between the two marks to see how tall *Dilong* was. Draw two more lines to create a rectangle. Now you can compare the sizes of all three tyrannosaurs. You may want to draw a figure that looks like *Dilong* inside the box.

Dilong

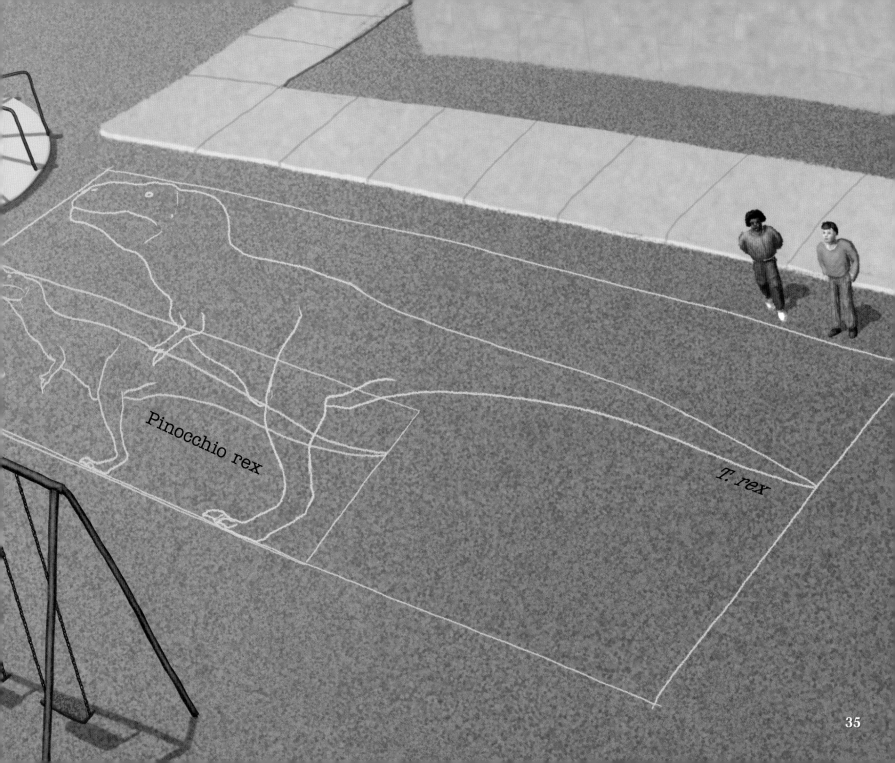

Pinocchio rex

T. rex

GLOSSARY

Asteroid—A large space rock.

Dinosaurs—A group of animals that lived mostly on land between 230 and 66 million years ago. They walked upright and had big arm muscles. The birds alive today developed from dinosaurs.

Fossil—Any evidence of past life, including teeth, bones, shells, plant imprints, footprints, nests, eggs, tooth marks, and dung.

Paleontologist—A scientist who studies dinosaurs and other kinds of fossils.

Skeleton—All the bones that make up an animal's body.

Tyrannosaurs—A group of meat-eating dinosaurs that walked on two legs.

WHERE TO SEE A *T. REX* & OTHER DINOSAURS:

- American Museum of Natural History, New York, NY
- Carnegie Museum of Natural History, Pittsburgh, PA
- Field Museum, Chicago, IL
- Natural History Museum, Los Angeles, CA
- New Mexico Museum of Natural History and Science, Albuquerque, NM
- Royal Tyrell Museum, Drumheller, Alberta, Canada
- Smithsonian Museum of Natural History, Washington DC

This book meets the Common Core State Standards for Science and Technical Subjects.

How TYRANNOSAURS Changed

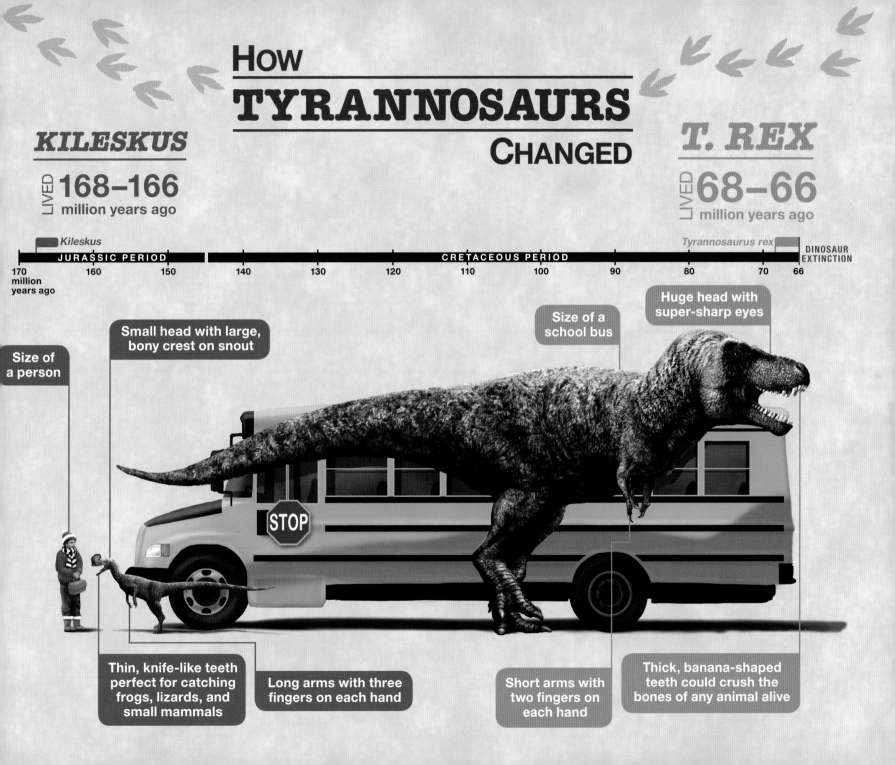

KILESKUS

LIVED **168–166** million years ago

T. REX

LIVED **68–66** million years ago

Kileskus		Tyrannosaurus rex
JURASSIC PERIOD	CRETACEOUS PERIOD	DINOSAUR EXTINCTION

170 million years ago | 160 | 150 | 140 | 130 | 120 | 110 | 100 | 90 | 80 | 70 | 66

Size of a person

Small head with large, bony crest on snout

Size of a school bus

Huge head with super-sharp eyes

STOP

Thin, knife-like teeth perfect for catching frogs, lizards, and small mammals

Long arms with three fingers on each hand

Short arms with two fingers on each hand

Thick, banana-shaped teeth could crush the bones of any animal alive

Be sure to look for all of these books in the **Let's-Read-and-Find-Out** Science series: